# DREAM CARS

## TOP STYLE AND PERFORMANCE

### DENIS J. HARRINGTON

**TODTRI**

This book was designed and produced by
TODTRI Book Publishers
P.O. Box 572, New York, NY 10116-0572
FAX : (212) 695-6984
e-mail : info@todtri.com


*Printed and bound in Indonesia by APP Printing*


ISBN 1-57717-007-5


Visit us on the web!
www.todtri.com


*Author:* Denis J. Harrington


*Publisher:* Robert M. Tod
*Editorial Director:* Elizabeth Loonan
*Book Designer:* Mark Weinberg
*Production Coordinator:* Heather Weigel
*Senior Editor:* Edward Douglas
*Project Editor:* Cynthia Sternau
*Assistant Editor:* Linda Greer
*Picture Researcher:* Laura Wyss
*Desktop Associate:* Michael Walther
*Typesetting:* Command-O, NYC

## PHOTO CREDITS

*All photographs by* Ron Kimball Sudios
*except pages 5-6:* Cindy Lewis Photography.

# CONTENTS

# INTRODUCTION

Deep within the human psyche lies the desire to be distinctive, to stand out in bold relief from the crowd. To the few people who have been endowed with special talents or abilities the achievement of this desire becomes a very real possibility. Most of us, however, must find alternative means to express our personalities; some chose to do this by driving a very special type of automobile: the dream car.

The rumble of a powerful motor imposes itself on the mass consciousness in a unique manner. Besides turning heads and eliciting envy, the resonant throbbing of pistons has succeeded in stirring the passions and the imagination of the public to such an extent that cultural patterns have been changed forever.

The glint of sunlight reflecting off a sleek, metallic shape coursing over a winding ribbon of asphalt with a throaty roar is a sight familiar to television viewers the world over. Auto advertisers spend millions of dollars every year to bring the sight and sound of their product into the homes of potential buyers. Exotic settings are frequent backdrops for upscale cars; the not-so-subtle message is that prosperous people drive them. The pitch implies that if you imitate success, it will happen. While this may not be true, the concept seldom fails to entice status-seekers through the showroom doors and into the automobile of their dreams.

The dream car syndrome has still another hook—a seductive appeal to the spirit of adventure that is native to us all. With this in mind auto manufacturers display their vehicles climbing rugged ascents, plowing through snow-choked terrain, fording streams, and cutting sandy furrows across desert wastes. Exhibitions of stunt driving offer further proof that the car is not just a vehicle for conveyance, but a machine capable of giving life to personal fantasies.

So it is that names such as Bronco, Cobra, Cougar, Jaguar, Firebird, Sting Ray, and Viper have been affixed to these gleaming composites of steel, glass, and plastic. This carefully contrived bit of imagery, tacked onto an already high-performance auto, has proven to be a very effective sales tool. Once the key turns in the ignition switch and the engine awakens with a growl, the psychology of marketing takes over. The driver

*1980 BMW M1*

*1957 T-Bird Convertible*

FOLLOWING PAGE:
1994 Lamborghini
Diablo V

*A powerful Ford V-8 engine housed in a pert British-made sports car chassis comprised the 1965 Sunbeam Tiger. Despite a petite appearance, this two-passenger roadster could exceed 100 miles per hour with a zero to 60 mph sprint speed worthy of its big cat namesake.*

is not just toeing an accelerator pedal, but prodding a great beast into action: Treaded claws paw the pavement and fendered shoulders hunch with the effort of movement. Dream cars, with their sloping lines and low-slung stance, imply an almost perceptible sense of danger.

The lure of speed is another factor dream car manufacturers have in their favor; there is something about defying the bonds of the natural physical order that has appealed to man for generations. Any number of people are interested in acquiring an automobile which can propel them along considerably faster than the law-enforcement establishment and good sense condone, and they want to bring the power and authority of that special machine under their control. If this means pushing the speedometer needle up to three digits in the process, then so be it. What is a 300- to 400-horsepower engine for, after all, if not to be put through its paces.

Debit financing and credit cards have enabled more people than ever to obtain their dream cars. And when those special wheels start showing their age there's usually an opportunity to trade up. Everything has a price, even love. But increasingly the attitude is: You only live once, go for it.

As a result, shiny new "missiles" in glaring reds and yellows with air foils and other racing features figure heavily in the metallic mix which clogs the traffic arteries of cities great and small. Today, corporate parking lots display as many upper-echelon automobiles in the general employees section as can be found in the executive area. What might be called dream car fever has become an epidemic.

The infection rate is so high that almost from the moment youngsters discard their tricycles for two-wheelers, they start entertaining thoughts of one day owning a car. By the time they graduate from high school, more often than not this goal has been achieved, and once they enter the work force the focus becomes more defined—it's not just a car any more, but *the car*. With the passing years this concept undergoes further changes, until the desired car must not only promise speed and adventure, but also serve as a unique symbol of its owner's personality and status.

*The 1952 Siata Spyder 208-S was right for its time—a sporty little runabout that looked good and handled well for a war-weary world just turning on to the concept of driving as a form of recreation and entertainment.*

# CHAPTER ONE

# IN THE BEGINNING

The modern sports car is a direct result of the ingenuity and experience gleaned from the builders and designers who served as the driving force behind Grand Prix racing in Europe immediately following World War II.

## EUROPEAN RACING MEN AND MACHINES

Perhaps the most dominant builder of road racers during the postwar period was Enzio Ferrari, a former driver turned designer who held forth as a fierce competitor and an innovator of considerable genius. His name still graces the most highly regarded sports cars in the world.

In 1948, Ferrari developed the Tipo 166, which was powered by a V-shaped twelve-cylinder engine and could attain a speed of 120 miles per hour. That year it won Italy's most important race, the Mille Miglia, and the Paris 12-hour competition. But in 1949, the car moved the Ferrari company to the head of the field with Formula One victories in the Grand Prix of Rosario and the famous Le Mans 24-hour endurance run.

From the very outset Ferdinand Porsche was concerned with designing cars for speed. His first effort, an electric-powered contrivance, had motors installed inside the hubcaps. It was the first front-wheel drive auto ever built. Later, Porsche produced a Mercedes racer for the Austrian Daimler Company. His car easily defeated the more highly regarded Alfa Romeo entry in Sicily's internationally renowned Targa Florio race. And, years before anyone else, Porsche experimented with air-cooled engines that had their cylinders arranged in a V-shaped pattern.

Early in 1947, Porsche and his son Ferry began work on a car that would be the first to bear the family name. It took the form of a streamlined, open two-seater, with the engine in back and a front-end fuel tank and spare-tire compartment. Dubbed the 356, it had a maximum speed of 86 miles per hour and a low center of gravity that aided the driving action of the rear wheels. From this design would evolve the famous Porsche 911, 928, and 959 series.

Before the war William Lyons concentrated on building cars of sporty design with expensive price tags. His pride and joy was the all-steel SS Jaguar, which could attain speeds in excess of 100 miles per hour and became a common sight at race courses throughout England and Europe. At the 1948 London Motor Show the Jaguar XK 120 roadster stole the limelight and caused a stir throughout the automotive world. By 1950 it had given way to the Jaguar C-type racer, which would successfully challenge Ferrari and Mercedes-Benz on the Formula One circuit.

The C-type models, with a top speed of 160 miles per hour, gave a good account of themselves at Le Mans with first place finishes in 1951 and 1953. When the D-type took over

*Chrysler executive Bob Rodgers had the youth market in mind when he put the 1955 C-300 model on the market. This limited edition hemi-hardtop with the Imperial grille had already established a national reputation on the stock car racing circuit.*

shortly thereafter, it won the famous endurance run three years in a row, in 1955, '56, and '57. In light of these racing achievements, Queen Elizabeth II knighted Lyons, whose Jaguar company then prevailed as the international leader of the sports car industry.

Karl Benz and Gottlieb Daimler are considered to be the founding fathers of the modern automobile. It was Benz who convinced his contemporaries that gasoline-powered engines were the wave of the future. Daimler took this innovation a step further when he patented a water-cooled engine. Benz didn't care for auto racing, considering it not only dangerous but undignified. Daimler, however, was of a different mind. He concentrated on building powerful engines and putting them in all manner of vehicles.

Despite his personal convictions, Benz felt compelled to contend with Daimler on the race course. The Daimler Mercedes was the top-rated Grand

Prix car when Benz began to compete. For a number of years the products of their engineering genius vied for racing honors, but eventually the Benz and Daimler groups merged to become Mercedes-Benz—and the rest is history.

The first race car to result from this marriage was the W25. It and succeeding models dominated the Formula One scene during the years immediately preceding World War II. After the fighting ended, Mercedes-Benz didn't return to racing until 1952; that year the company's 300 SL gullwing design won three Grand Prix events. In 1955, a 300 SL went out of control at Le Mans and killed more than eighty spectators. At the close of the season Mercedes-Benz officially quit the Formula One circuit; the firm would not resume racing until 1987.

*The Mercedes 300SL Gullwing was the first super sports car of the postwar era. Designers did not get their inspiration from a gull in flight but used a concept common to the manner in which the cockpits of fighter planes were opened.*

*Among the most popular Porches of its era was the 1959 Speedster. It sold like hot cakes in America after Paul Newman starred opposite the racy model in the film* Haper.

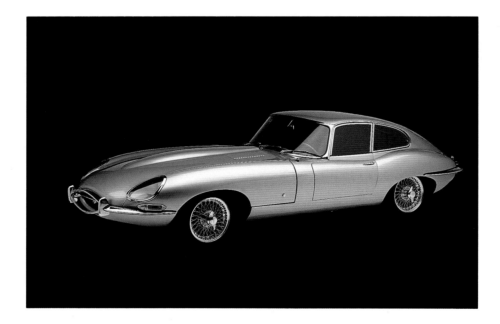

*A success right off the production line, the 1961 Jaguar E-Type took the public by storm after the Geneva Motor Show, combining good looks, stunning performance, and affordability.*

*In 1962, the Ferrari GTO evolved from the SWB Berlinetta. The new GTO model featured exterior cooling vents for the engine as well as the front and rear brakes. Form and function were perfectly united for maximum performance.*

## AMERICA JOINS THE FIELD

Henry Ford, founder of the Ford Motor Company, never showed much of an interest in auto racing, only dabbling with a variety of relatively primitive machines during the early years of the sport. But his grandson, Henry Ford II, had a much different view of racing and its value in marketing consumer automobiles. In order to compete favorably with the established car lines from Europe, he reasoned, it would first be necessary to do well against those manufacturers' products on the Formula One circuit.

Ford initially attempted to buy the Ferrari company, which had been a major Grand Prix force for years, but Enzo Ferrari refused to sell. Next,

*The 1962 Chevrolet Corvette convertible represented the end of the opening era for this model. A decade of Corvette history had been accomplished, and, a year later, significant changes in structure and design would be implemented.*

Ford sought to take over race car designer Colin Chapman's Lotus organization in England. Again, this proved impossible. Ultimately, Ford assumed control of Lola, a small British race car firm which already used the American V-8 engine. The next step involved hiring the best technical people available. When this was accomplished, the quest to bring Formula One eminence and prestige to the United States began in earnest.

American engineers designed the Ford GT40 Mk I for the assault on the company's principal target, the Le Mans 24-hour endurance run. The "GT" stood for Grand Touring, while "40" indicated the car's height in inches. It measured 13 feet, 9 inches in length, was 5 feet, 10 inches wide, and weighed 1,835 pounds.

In 1964, the GT40s were the fastest entries at Le Mans, but mechanical problems prevented them from being serious contenders. The following year the cars again broke down after taking the lead early on, but Ford's determination paid off in 1966, when the GT40 Mk II took the checkered flag ahead of the pack.

A year later the GT40 Mk III also finished first. Satisfied, Ford handed over control of the Formula One racing program to John Wyer, manager of the independent Gulf racing team. Wyer went on to win at Le Mans in both 1968 and 1969 using the same GT40 Mk IV.

People the world over now wanted the street version of the fabulous Le Mans champion GT40. The engine mounted behind the cockpit had a 500-horsepower capacity and propelled the sheet steel monocoque (honeycomb) fiberglass body from 0 to 60 miles per hour in 4.5 seconds and to 100 miles per hour in less than 9 seconds. It was the dawn of a new era.

*In 1956, the Ford T-Bird had the spare tire fixed behind the trunk on what's called a continental mount. But this arrangement made the car tail-heavy, so more structural changes were in store the following year.*

*Known as America's favorite family car, the 1962 Chevrolet Impala SS had it all—from open-air elegance to a strong power-pack under the hood. Its boxy but stream-lined design was meant to steal the spotlight from the com-peting Ford Falcon model.*

The 1963 Corvette "Split Window" was one of the most popular models Chevrolet ever built. Demand far outstripped supply, as only 10,594 of these cars were built. Even today, this vintage model of the famous sports car is much sought after.

Chevrolet designer Bill Mitchell got his inspiration for the 1963 Corvette "Split Window" while on a fishing trip to Florida. There he saw a graceful but powerful stingray alongside the boat and promptly decided to borrow the name for his new line of sports cars.

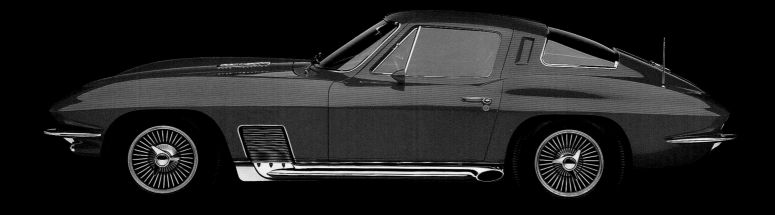

## FROM TRACK TO SHOWROOM

With the success of his racing program Ferrari was able to build a large, international clientele for the passenger car business. First, this meant expanding from workshop auto construction to mass-production methods. Then the company began buying parts from suppliers instead of making them themselves. Finally, it became necessary to use a network of dealerships to meet marketing demands.

In 1954, Ferrari introduced the 250 series. The pace-setters of this breed were the Testarossa and the GT Spyder; of these two models the most coveted was the Testarossa. Its name means "red-head"— the engine top was painted red so it wouldn't be confused with other makes during the building process. Once off the assembly line, however, the Testarossa stood alone both in design and performance. It had a top speed of 176 miles per hour and could go from 0 to 100 miles per hour in 14.1 seconds.

Not to be outdone, Mercedes-Benz used its hard-won racing knowledge to develop a luxury car for the international market; this marked the inception of what was soon to become the firm's famous 300 series. In 1954, the 300 SL coupe commandeered the spotlight at the New York auto show. Like its Grand Prix counterpart, the stylish two-seater had doors which opened overhead in gullwing fashion. This unique facet, along with a six-cylinder engine capable of producing speeds in excess of 150 miles per hour, caught the fancy of the automotive world. It was voted the most exciting sports car of the decade.

Hardly willing to take a back seat, Jaguar kept improving the lines and powerplant of its already classic XK 120 roadster. After a headline debut at the 1948 London auto show the sleek sports car gave birth to the XK 140 and XK 150 versions. The more glamorous of

*Auto experts agree that the Corvette just kept getting better every year. The 1964 proto-type model had dropped the rear split-window design from the previous model and boasted markedly increased horsepower from its fuel-injection engine.*

The 1965 Ford AC Cobra
readily shows the British
influence in its chassis
design. The rounded lines
and broad nose are undeni-
ably those of the old Ace roadster, but its powerpack and
infrastructure were definitely
American and innovative.

A General Motors ban on
drag racing programs as a
sales promotion tool seriously
threatened the market arrival of
the racy 1964 Pontiac GTO, but
quick-thinking company executives
featured the high-performance
model as a Le Mans option and
it safely passed corporate muster.

*The 1966 Corvette 427 was of classic fastback design with a 450-horsepower engine option. Referred to as the "plastic fantastic," it reigned as one of the most notable high-profile sports cars of the era and did much to enhance the Sting Ray image at home and abroad.*

*Minimal but concise changes in design to the cab and hood areas gave the 1967 Corvette Sting Ray a more aristocratic bearing. This model featured electrically powered covers which drew back and allowed the headlights to pop up for night driving, an innovation that persists as a "design option" to this day.*

these offspring was the XK 150, which hit the market in 1957 with both hardtop and convertible options. Broader and more luxurious than its XK 120 ancestor, the XK 150 had a wraparound windshield and an adjustable steering column, both innovations at that time. It could top 130 miles per hour and reach 60 miles per hour from a standing start in 7.6 seconds.

Although Ferdinand Porsche died in 1951, the company's cars continued to bear his distinctive stamp of genius. But it was his son Ferry and their associate Karl Rabe who moved the family name to the forefront of the auto industry during the postwar period. Their efforts produced the 356 roadster which attracted the attention of sports car enthusiasts the world over. It had a rear-mounted motor with horizontally opposed cylinders, and could attain speeds of better than 100 miles per hour. The interior featured a padded dashboard and comfortable, upholstered seats.

Racing standards for efficiency and performance dominated the construction of commercial cars in the early 1950s, but a concern for creature comforts and visual appeal strongly asserted itself during the middle and latter phases of the decade. It stood to reason that power would always be a strong factor in marketing strategy, but designers also realized most buyers wanted a vehicle they could be proud to drive. And so automakers set about giving aesthetics a more prominent place in their production philosophy.

## ONLY FOR THE RICH AND FAMOUS

The Volkswagen was specifically designed for the masses, and it was a car that the average person could afford to own. But, as a rule, passenger vehicles weren't produced with the person on the street in mind during the years immediately following the war.

A classic example was the 1956 BMW 507, an exotic-looking sports coupe which its German manufacturer built especially for the American market. This high-performance machine featured a lightweight aluminum engine that could power its tubular steel chassis upwards of 120 miles per hour. Unfortunately, it was priced well beyond the reach of middle America.

In 1948, the Jaguar XK 120 held forth as the sensation of the sports car industry. It was a hand-built, two-passenger roadster with an aluminum body and classic racing lines. Because only a small

*The 1965 275 GTB Ferrari was the amateur racer's dream car. Moderately priced but still a perfect blend of form and function, this model allowed owners to look the sport on the road during the week and play at the club track on the weekend.*

number were produced, they immediately became collectors' items and their market value skyrocketed. Film star Clark Gable managed to acquire one through his affiliation with company president Sir William Lyons—it took that kind of clout and money to own one of these classic beauties.

When General Motors spent several hundred million dollars to retool its Buick design the result was the 1957 Roadmaster, measuring a massive 17 feet, 11 inches long and 6 feet wide. It possessed a 300-horsepower engine, a dynaflow transmission with pitched blades that changed angles like those of an airplane propeller, and lots of chrome stripping. But the public took neither to the car's futuristic design nor to its out-of-the-world price.

America's dream car of the 1950s was the Cadillac Eldorado convertible. Standard equipment on the 1953 model included a Hydra-Matic transmission, hydraulic windows, a search radio, tinted glass, vanity and side mirrors, and a cast-iron V-8 engine which could generate speeds exceeding 110 miles per hour. Its major shortcoming was a $7,750 take-home tag, which only wealthy individuals such as Marilyn Monroe and President Dwight D. Eisenhower could afford.

The 1959 Caddy convertible housed a 325-horsepower engine with a cast-iron block, five main bearings, and hydraulic valve lifters, and could also eclipse 100 miles per hour. Other features were a wrap-around windshield, power brakes and steering, electronically operated seats, windows, and trunk, and a pair of exaggerated tail fins. World champion prize fighter Sugar Ray Robinson owned a flamingo-colored model, while another one of pink hue starred with actor Clint Eastwood in a film aptly titled *Pink Cadillac*.

Contrasting sharply in size and design was the British Bentley R-Type Continental. The elegantly tailored 1952 model had a beautiful detailed dashboard and a sleek, largely aluminum body. Advertised as a "modern magic carpet," it could do 115 miles per hour and reach 60 miles per hour in less than 14 seconds. But all this styling and power pushed the sales price to $18,000, making it the most expensive production car in the world.

Much the same scenario applied to the French Facel line of sports cars, widely admired and sought after during this era. Sumptuously outfitted and meticulous in every detail, these glossy confections could attain a top speed of 140 miles per hour and sprint to 100 miles per hour in just 17 seconds. But their cost confined ownership to such monied celebrities as Ringo Starr, Ava Gardner, Danny Kaye, Tony Curtis, Joan Collins, and Pablo Picasso.

Despite these displays of excess, automakers were already expanding production of their middle-range cars to accommodate the average wage-earner. During the next decade this market would be exploited as it had never been before.

*In 1967 the Ford Mustang truly became a muscle car. Design changes made it lower, longer, wider, and much more powerful than its predecessors, and it housed a monster 390-cubic-inch, V-8 engine which gave it speed to burn.*

CHAPTER TWO

# Mania for the Masses

With economic conditions improving almost daily in both the United States and Europe, working men and women began to seriously consider the challenge of leisure time.

## The Cult Years

No more visible means of expressing one's improved financial status existed during the period dubbed the "swinging '60s" than the exhibiting of a late-model automobile; if it was one of the genuinely coveted makes, so much the better.

In the parlance of the car manufacturing trade, the decade from 1960 to 1969 is referred to as the "cult years." Mass-production methods made it possible to build attractive, high-performance vehicles which were within the means of the general public. Further abetting the rise of mass motorism was the low cost of gasoline, which sold for as little as fifteen cents a gallon, and the fact that stringent speed limits had not yet been imposed on open road traffic. These conditions served as an open invitation to put the pedal to the metal and let fantasies go into overdrive.

Sensing the moment, automakers on both sides of the Atlantic delved deep into their collective imaginations to produce suitable machines for the age. British builders exported the sports car mentality worldwide, while their American counterparts brought forth power-packed machines with innovative styling that added a guttural roar to the other sounds already filling the urban atmosphere.

European contributions to the roadster craze bore names like Jaguar E-Type, MGB Tourer, Austin-Healey 3000, Triumph TR, and Daimler SP250 Dart (England); Ferrari 250 GT SWB, Ferrari 275 GTB/4, Ferrari 365 GTB/4 Daytona, Ferrari Dino 246 GT, Lamborghini Miura, and Maserati Ghibli (Italy); Mercedes-Benz 280 SL and Porsche 356B (Germany); Renault Alpine A110 (France); and Volvo P1800 (Sweden). Japan also jumped into this new market with the Datsun 240Z and Toyota 2000 GT.

Responding to the foreign challenge, the American auto industry produced such sports cars as the American Motors AMX, Chevrolet Corvette Sting Ray, Chevrolet Camaro RS convertible, Chevrolet Mako Shark, Ford GT40 Mk I, II, III, and IV, and Pontiac Firebird/Trans Am. But other makes which lapped over into this classification included the Dodge Charger R/T (a modified road racer), Ford Mustang Boss, Ford Thunderbird Sports Roadster, Oldsmobile Toronado, Plymouth Sport Fury, Plymouth Road Runner, Pontiac GTO, and Studebaker Avanti.

Nearly all American automakers put out hot versions of the regular models in their production lineup. And they, too, used racing prototypes as the basis for developing the top-selling sports machines. Prominent examples of this transfer process were the winged Dodge Charger Daytona and Ford's Mustang Boss 429.

*Few cars got more publicity than the Pontiac Firebird, which was featured in the popular TV detective series* The Rockford Files. *Shown here is the 1967 convertible version, the manufacturer's first "pony car."*

During this decade more people were able to derive more excitement from owning a car than at any other time in modern history. Contributing to this unique era were a minimum of government restrictions on motorized overland travel, low fuel prices, alternate methods of financing purchases, and a plethora of high-performance, attractive vehicles far different from anything that had previously been available. No wonder that the models of the 1960s have become particularly prized possessions of today's dream car fanciers!

## IMAGES IN SONG AND CELLULOID

Cars play a prominent role in people's lives for reasons other than transportation, and, frequently, they can be the focal point of an especially nostalgic interlude in an ordinary life. The entertainment industry has long been attuned to this quirk in the human condition, and so it is that cars have found their way into the lyrics of popular songs and played prominent supporting roles in films of all genres.

"Fun, fun, fun until daddy took her T-Bird away," rhapsodized the Beach Boys in their 1960s release entitled "Fun, Fun, Fun." They also serenaded the Chevy Corvette with their hit "In My Car." Next came "Little Deuce Coupe," the reference being to racy two-seater sports cars across the board, and "409," a tribute to the Chevrolet Bel Air 409. All these renditions made the Top 40 charts and were oriented toward young drivers interested in drag racing and other fast-paced motor pursuits.

In 1971, singer Don McLean's "American Pie" called to mind a Chevrolet of that era. A few years later the noted rock group The Eagles lamented the vagaries of the law and a street-burning Maserati. Natalie Cole crooned "Pink Cadillac" to a lofty place on the charts in 1988. And country star Alan Jackson did the same for his 1994 ballad about a hard-charging Mercury Cougar.

Several movies have showcased cars to advantage through the years, but some productions actually featured a vehicle as an integral part of the plot. In 1964, the Aston Martin DB4 made its debut in the James Bond film *Goldfinger*; and two decades later the V-8 Volante version of the Aston Martin was still on the job in *The Living Daylights*.

During the 1970s the Dodge Charger R/T got more screen mileage than any other car. It was the star of a 9-minute chase scene in the movie *Bullit*, and it also played a major role in a fad film titled *Vanishing Point*. But its greatest exposure came in the highly popular television series "The Dukes of Hazard."

European makes to enjoy top billing during this period were the Ferrari Dino 246 GT, Alfa Romeo 1300 Junior Spider, and Volvo P1800. The Dino appeared front and center in the television series "The Persuaders," while the 1300 Junior Spider was the ride of choice in the Dustin Hoffman film *The Graduate*.

*A leather-rimmed steering wheel, floor shift, grooved dashboard, and bucket seats put the 1970 Pontiac Trans Am among the sportiest of its breed. This model was a Hollywood favorite, and appeared in a number of films.*

## REVISIONS, RESTRICTIONS, AND REDUCTIONS

Following the idyllic automotive decade of the 1960s, government legislation put the brakes on both car design and technology. Mandatory speed limits became commonplace for both urban and rural driving. Radar surveillance was instituted primarily to curtail high-speed traffic along freeways and other limited-access thoroughfares. Cars with sleek lines, racing stripes, and bright colors routinely attracted the attention of police on the prowl.

*The 1968 Ford Mustang (California Special Red) enjoyed sales success both at home and in Europe. It featured windows which could be rolled completely out of sight, giving it the airiness of a convertible.*

Auto insurers also began to more carefully define accident-prone motorists, who were placed in higher premium brackets and often had their policies canceled after receiving an excessive number of citations. Public campaigns to encourage more responsibility and restraint behind the wheel became widespread. Young people were required to take safe-driving instruction classes as part of the regular high school curriculum before they could obtain an operator's permit.

But nothing curtailed the dash and drive of the automakers' art quite like government restrictions aimed at reducing air pollution and fuel consumption. During the 1970s long lines of cars at gas stations were not unusual due to supply shortages. For a time the prospect of rationing loomed large as legislators considered how best to insure the most equitable use of dwindling reserves.

Then Congress enacted a clean-air act designed to reduce the amount of toxic emissions into the atmosphere. One of the safeguards imposed called for downsizing auto engine capacity and output. Car engineers were forced to alter their specifications, and the end result was a definite retreat from the freewheeling mentality which had prevailed only a decade earlier.

What rolled off the assembly lines in this era came laden with emission control pipery and all manner of safety devices. These additions made automobiles bulkier, heavier, and generally less efficient. As might be expected, the sporting genre suffered most from these encumbrances. Overall, new car sales fell off while used car sales rose sharply. Enthusiasts as well as buyers interested only in acquiring the best ride possible turned to the past for what had proven to be tried and true.

Detroit automakers and their European counterparts found themselves wedged between a rock and a hard place by the unexpected government intervention. At first, they attempted to compensate for their products' general loss of appeal with more technological improvements. Considerable effort was expended to provide a smoother and more enjoyable driving experience as well as better gas mileage. They succeeded in achieving these goals, but still the public was not drawn to the sterile designs which resulted from the new restrictions.

Finally, industry leaders came to their collective senses and awoke to the fact that style was as important as performance in the marketplace. So began the movement away from the prevailing safe and staid philosophy to a more sane approach. The Jaguar company showed the way by incorporating some frills of former days with a very subtle hint of futurism. Other manufacturers followed suit and a new automotive age was born.

*FOLLOWING PAGE: No model better fit the cult car age of the 1960s than the 1967 Lamborghini Miura. Beautifully constructed and cat-quick with a top speed of 175 miles per hour, it was widely considered to be the most desirable car in the marketplace.*

*Dodge was the last major American auto manufacturer to enter the pony car race with its 1970 RT Challenger. Only 356 of these models with the "Street Hemi" engine were built that year.*

## WHEELS ACROSS THE WORLD

The cars of the 1980s featured chrome, emblems, padded dashboards, upholstered interiors, rakish lines, and other nuances reminiscent of the models of twenty years earlier. At the same time hooded headlights, exotic dials, and hubcaps with garish crests and glittering spokes hinted of things to come. It was this mix that served to turn on a new generation of car buyers.

Ferrari's engineers now took the lead. The 1984 Testarossa was built specifically for the American market and conformed to all safety and emissions standards. Unlike competing sports models it was unusually wide, measuring 6 feet across, with a low-slung stance and a twelve-cylinder engine which generated a top speed of 181 miles per hour.

In 1986, the Ferrari 328 GTB took the automotive world by storm. With a powerful V-8 engine and innovative design, it was the builder's best-selling car of the decade. A year later the Ferrari company produced the F40 model. Metals, ceramics, and glass were fused to construct the body, and a clear plastic sheath covered the rear-mounted V-8 engine. It was the first production roadster to be capable of 200 miles per hour.

The Japanese invasion of the American and European markets began in earnest with the 1972 Honda Civic 1200. In 1976, the Accord established itself as the firm's most popular model, and two years later, the Prelude joined the fray. With the onset of the 1980s Honda opened a production plant in the United States, and things haven't been the same since.

*Pontiac continued to ply the youth market with its 1968 GTO convertible option. Described somewhat nonsensically as "A Pontiac in a saber-toothed tiger skin," it featured a number of style changes including disappearing windshield wipers.*

Nissan's famed Z-Car line also moved the automotive industry in a new direction. A special tenth-anniversary ZX10 model was offered on a limited basis to kick off the '80s version of the series. In 1982, the 289 ZX boasted a turbocharger option which put it on a par with other high-performance sports cars in the world market. The ZX model changed very little during the remainder of the decade, but in 1990, the 300 ZX displayed a much sportier design and a stronger powerpack than ever before.

All the while Toyota was also making an indelible impression on the international scene. The Corolla subcompact sedan, the company's flag bearer, can be legitimately categorized as a true world car, for it is sold in more than 130 countries with profits nearing the twenty-million-dollar level. Vying for equal status are the Camry coupe and the stylish Supra Turbo sports model.

During the early 1990s it became evident to American automakers that in order to be competitive, their cars would have to rival foreign imports not only in cost but also in fuel efficiency, compact design, and overall durability. Thus it was that luxury sedans and town cars quickly shrunk in size and shed their broad, blocky shapes for a more rounded, smoother appearance.

Today, low-profile, high-density cars fit into smaller parking places but not necessarily smaller price ranges. Rear-mounted air foils have become almost standard equipment for sports models, along with truncated backsides and protuberant noses. Even the multiple-passenger sedans are abandoning any pretense of conservatism in favor of more exotic angles, curves, and enticing colors.

Auto manufacturing has become truly international, and it is not uncommon now for companies from different countries to jointly design, produce, and market a car for worldwide distribution.

*In 1973 the Dino Ferrari GT still did not carry the company's famous rearing-horse insignia. This model was radically changed from previous editions in both design and powerpack with a new 90 degree V-8 engine.*

Like its ancestors, the 1976 Lamborghini JHarma turned heads and defied conventional engineering wisdom and design. But this was naturally in keeping with company tradition.

The 1971 Dodge Challenger continued to do just that in the pony car competition. Many auto experts lauded it as being the best of its breed.

Teams of specialists were used to construct the 1990 Porsche Speedster. Among them were craftsmen, mechanics, body men, and upholsterers who had produced the first 356 Speedster more than thirty years earlier.

A leading auto magazine described the 1968 Corvette 327 as a car that could take you on a trip without going anywhere. It was sleek and curvaceous and officially became known as the Stingray, not the Sting Ray.

*Sweeping lines and a high-angle hatchback design characterized the 1987 Ford concept 2000 GT model. It was a marked departure from the traditional look of this make, particularly with its nose-down racing stance.*

*The 1989 Ford Thunderbird SC displayed the more rounded shape and lines this model assumed in the 1980s. Called the wind-shape look, it not only afforded better aerodynamics and handling but increased sales as well.*

*FOLLOWING PAGE:*
*By 1991 the Mitsubishi 3000 GT had established itself as the leading Japanese sports import on the American market. It had looks, reasonable power, smooth performance, and the right price tag.*

*In keeping with company policy, the 1989 Ford Saleen Mustang was quieter, smoother, faster, and better handling than the previous year, but still kept its signature look.*

In 1989 the Lamborghini Countach experienced a number of interior design improvements. Of these the most important were enlarging the driving compartment and adding electronically controlled seats and a more effective ventilation system.

The 1989 Lamborghini Countach displayed a rear deck air foil reminiscent of a Grand Prix road racer. With a glistening black body and swing-wing doors this model was a show-stopper wherever it went.

*After two years of production the 1990 Ferrari F-40 had undergone only negligible changes in design. Its aerodynamics forced air along the body and into the rear brake cooling vents.*

*Like all of its line the 1990 Ferrari F-40 was loaded with race car technology and very little driver comfort. In essence, the engineers built it for competition on the track and only secondarily for town traffic.*

*The 1991 Callaway Speedster was the brainchild conversion of twin-turbo builder Ely Reeves Callaway. It made its debut to public acclaim at the Los Angeles Auto Show of that year.*

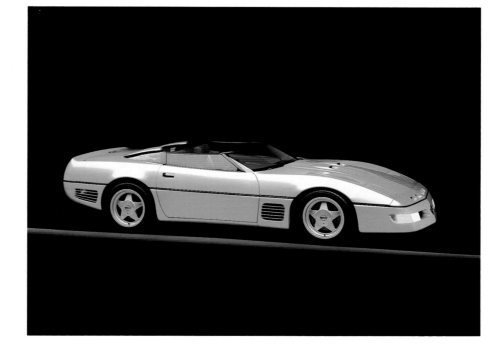

*The 1991 Callaway Corvette was the first conversion of this line which did not house a twin turbo powerpack. It used a super-aspirated Corvette LT-5 V-8 (the standard ZR-1 engine) souped up to generate 465 horsepower.*

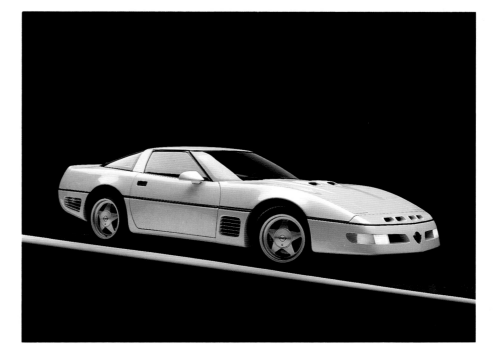

*The 1989 Porsche Speedster was a labor of love for the designers and engineers. It resulted from the "homogenizing" of two prototype models, and assembly took place under top secret security.*

In 1991, the Dodge Stealth
rolled off the assembly line for
the first time as the company
sought to revitalize its line.
Since then, this model had
enjoyed ever-growing public
acceptance and acclaim.

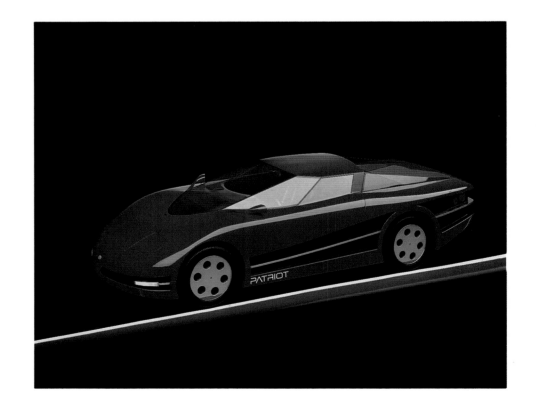

The 1992 Patriot was the
product of specialty builder
Adrian Corbett of Lompoc,
California. Its design easily
qualifies as exotic, with the
windows being particularly
futuristic in concept.

*In only the second year of production the 1990 Nissan 300ZX, here shown as a convertible conversion, had already established itself as one of the most beautiful sports cars ever built.*

*The product of a Florida specialty builder, the 1990 Consulier GTP combined an extremely lightweight body with a powerful turbo engine; its speed and lines were similar to those of GTP race cars.*

*The 1992 BMW 850i was a tribute to good German engineering and craftsmanship—so much so that few adjustments had to be made on later models. It looked good and was fun to drive.*

*Though sleek and attractive, the 1993 Acura NSX had a
few problems. Its transmission gears didn't mesh and,
on occasion, were noisy. Also, the wheels proved to be a
bit small for the turning base and handling was difficult.*

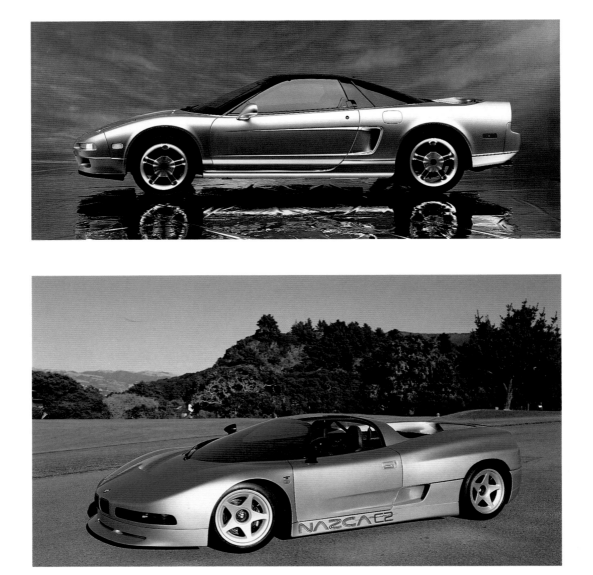

*The 1993 BMW NAZCA CZ Spider model grew out of
the German manufacturer's continuing quest to rival the
Japanese Z-Car invasion of the European market. Its beetle-
like design was meant to ensure a better center of gravity.*

*The 1986 Ferrari Testarosa evidenced no significant
structural or design alterations from the original model
of two years before. When a car looked this good, the builder
reasoned, there simply wasn't any reason to change it.*

The 1995 Ford GT-90 is a prototype of a sports car with a V-12 engine. Inside the driver's compartment the colors are navy blue upholstery and Art Deco silver and black for the control panel. This model was inspired by the Ford GT-40 Le Mans champions of the 1960s.

CHAPTER THREE

# SPORTS CARS WITH ATTITUDES

Sports car production has become the most competitive aspect of the automaking industry. An ever-increasing amount of money, time, and talent is devoted to developing ego machines to capture the public imagination. Looks, speed, and comfort continue to be the factors of prime importance to buyers in determining the desired make, and now the variety is greater than ever before.

## 1996—PICK OF THE GLITZ

The sports cars currently drawing the lion's share of attention from both critics and connoisseurs are the Porsche 911 Turbo, Ferrari F355, Acura NSX-T, Toyota Supra Turbo, Chevrolet Corvette, Mazda RX-7 Turbo, Nissan 300 ZX Turbo, Dodge Stealth Turbo, and Dodge Viper R/T10.

The superstar of the lot is the Porsche 911 Turbo, considered to have the most sophisticated mechanical system of its breed. With a maximum speed of 177.32 miles per hour, it is one of the fastest cars in the world: From a standing start it can reach 60 miles per hour in just 3.5 seconds and 100 miles per hour in only 8.6 seconds.

The Ferrari F355 is described as the most beautiful of all the models the company currently produces. It's a convertible containing technology refined on the racing circuit and comes with a flat, streamlined underside similar to those of Formula One cars. The engine has a 375-horsepower capacity and a top speed of 130 miles per hour.

A removable roof enables the Acura NSX-T to become a convertible—of sorts. The car has an automatic transmission instead of the manual shift usually found in most roadsters. This reduces engine output slightly, but the 252-horsepower motor can still produce 162 miles per hour on the straightaway.

Broad and muscular, the Toyota Supra Turbo boasts a six-speed manual transmission which provides for a strong accelerating thrust. Despite a modest V6-T setup it can go from a standing start to 60 miles per hour in a respectable 5 seconds and reach 155 miles per hour flat out.

In 1997, the Chevrolet Corvette will undergo a complete style overhaul. As a way of bidding farewell to this historic line Chevy has released two Corvette versions for 1996—the Collector's Edition and the Grand Sport. Only one thousand of the Grand Sport makes are for purchase. Standard equipment includes bucket seats, a Z51 suspension system, and a 330-horse-power, V-8 engine which can attain a speed of 162 miles per hour.

Like the Corvette, the Nissan 300 ZX is expected to become history soon. This most appealing sports car has undergone little if any upgrading in recent times, especially with regard to its V-6 twin turbo engine.

Like others of its class the 1993 Mazda RX7 RI ran with all the precision and smoothness of a Swiss watch. Its clean, flowing lines and moderate pricing made it a popular buy in both the United States and Europe.

Exotic says it all for the 1994 Bizzarini. Its bathtub configuration and baroque body design speak of Romanesque passion and innovation as well as a disdain for tradition.

The 1993 Dodge Viper has been called a "Naked Gun"—meaning it was an ultra fast, good-looking toy with little attention given to such matters as passenger comfort and practicality of design.

*The 1994 Alfa Romeo Spider combined a wonderfully responsive engine, fine road balance, easy handling, and classic good looks to maintain its well-deserved cult car reputation.*

The Mazda RX-7 continues to rank high among its sports car contemporaries while still utilizing a rotary-style engine, in this case a 1.3 twin turbo powerpack. This is a high-performance machine in every respect, with near racing capabilities. A word of caution to would-be owners—it requires delicate handling at high speeds.

At 3,000 pounds the Dodge Stealth R/T Turbo is the heaviest of its breed, but also one of the easiest to manage. Four-wheel drive and a squat build give this model excellent all-weather road adherence. These safety factors and an attractive appearance make the Stealth a very enticing purchase.

The Dodge Viper RT/10 is essentially a one-dimensional vehicle. It's designed to fly with little concern for utility, and sounds like a boiler factory when fully exercising its powerful 420-horsepower, V-10 engine.

## FANCY ODDS AND ENDS

Dream car enthusiasts seeking something a bit offbeat can now choose from a number of superb options. Prominent among these are the BMW 8 Series, Bugatti EB 110, Jaguar XJS, Lamborghini Diablo VT, Mercedes-Benz SL, and Renault Sport Spider.

The BMW 850CSi is the largest and most powerful coupe of the Bavarian manufacturer's line and commands the highest price tag of the lot. It possesses a 376-horsepower, V-12 engine and a six-speed manual mode transmission which combine to generate an all-out effort of 155 miles per hour. (This model is not currently available in the United States.)

Exotic is the best word to describe the Bugatti EB 110. The parent company only recently began to prepare the version of this car which will be marketed in America. It's to have a 600-horsepower, V-12 engine with a top speed of 215 miles per hour. Advertising claims say it can go from start to 60 miles per hour in a breathtaking 3.3 seconds; the asking price is equally breathtaking.

Some experts argue that the Jaguar XJS convertible is not a sports car. They say it's simply too large for this category at nearly 4,000 pounds and 16 feet long. But Jaguar just doesn't make bad automobiles, and this glimmering droptop is no exception. The 223-horsepower engine purrs like a cat and has a quick, subtle response to the accelerator pedal.

A real knockout by any measure is the Lamborghini Diablo VT. It's designed to eat up the miles with an almost casual display of energy while exhibiting almost no vibrations or tremors. The 492-horsepower, V-12 engine can produce straightaway speeds of 200 miles per hour and a 0 to 60 dash time of 4 seconds flat, but it still handles and corners well due to a low-slung stance and four-wheel drive. The doors to this two-seater open up and forward in butterfly fashion, which is guaranteed to turn heads everywhere.

All things considered, the Mercedes-Benz SL convertible has to be the pick of this imposing group, with a fully automated top, brakes that activate indi-

*FOLLOWING PAGE:
The 1994 Ford Mustang
GT convertible displayed
less of a racing car profile
and more of a sportier
European look than was
the case in previous years.
Competition and changing
times prompted this change.*

*Like its predecessors, the 1995
Aston Martin DB7 continued
to be the choice of royalty,
celebrities, and the monied
classes worldwide. It also
prevailed as the official car
of the James Bond film series.*

vidually to reduce the potential for sliding or skidding, standard-size air bags contained in both doors, and a stabilizing weight of better than 4,000 pounds. The 389-horsepower, V-12 engine can do 155 miles per hour and sprint from start to 60 miles per hour in 6 seconds. Aiding this powerpack is an electronically operated five-speed transmission along with an on-board computer and a new fuel injection system—all state-of-the-art German engineering.

"Unique" best describes the Renault Sport Spider. It's a miniature, street-legal racer with neck-snapping acceleration. At only 1,742 pounds, it possesses

*The 1994 Bugatti EB110 coupe was in keeping with the company's devotion to building exceptional cars and marketing them at absolutely unaffordable prices.*

unusual maneuverability but still tracks well given its squat stance and good balance. The 150-horsepower engine generates road speeds of 130 miles per hour. It has no side windows or roof, and a large roll bar comes as standard equipment. Taking the place of a windshield is an ingeniously designed wind deflector which effectively protects the passengers from airborne elements. Bluntly put, the Renault Sport Spider is a fun car for those who are not particularly faint of heart.

## THE NEXT BEST THING

If money is a consideration there are several sports coupes on the market today which can serve as significant statement-making vehicles.

High on the list of desirable buys in this category are the Honda Civic Si Coupe, Volkswagen Golf GT1, Chevrolet Cavalier 29-Z24, Mazda MX-3,

Nissan 200SX SE-R, Dodge/Plymouth Neon Sport Coupe, Saturn SC2, Ford Escort GT, and Toyota Paseo.

The Honda Civic Si Coupe is generally considered to be the class of this field. In the 1996 model comfort has become more of a factor than in past years, with better headroom and a bit broader body. A 127-horsepower engine provides good acceleration and a sound, functional ride.

Strong performance has always been a trademark of Volkswagen, and the Golf GT1 is no exception. The 115-horsepower engine affords a quiet, steady drive with sufficient get-up-and-go when needed. Despite its small size there are ample, uncramped accommodations in the passenger area.

Unlike its contemporaries, the Chevrolet Cavalier offers a full array of standard equipment, including dual air bags, anti-lock brakes, and power-tilt steering. The 120-horsepower engine can generate a top speed of 109 miles per hour. Although small, it still corners well due to its low center of gravity.

Always popular, the Mazda MX-3 has one of the most familiar and attractive configurations worldwide of any car in its genre. Besides good looks it offers reasonable creature comforts and dependability, with a 105-horsepower engine capable of attaining 100 miles per hour.

The Nissan 200SX E-R continues to be among the leaders in road adherence and comfort. Its durability and construction have been improved from previous years with a particularly precise and reactive gearshift setup. The 140-horsepower engine tends to be a mite noisy at times, but its performance is consistently satisfactory.

Sound performance and strong traction mark the Dodge/Plymouth Neon Sport Coupe in its second year of production. This is a racy little model with a 150-horsepower engine and a top speed capability of approximately 121 miles per hour.

*The 1994 Chevrolet Camaro Z-28 cut a handsome figure with its compact but stream-lined shape. A six-speed manual transmission and a powerful V-8 engine gave this model both strong acceleration and staying power.*

Creature comforts marked the 1994 Chevrolet Corvette Convertible. It featured leather bucket seats and a leather-wrapped steering wheel along with a center console, tinted glass, and ample leg room.

Unlike other street-legal cars the 1995 Ferrari 355 Spyder offers some interior elegance for the passengers. The dashboard and controls are done in black and silver and the seating is comfortable—but wear ear plugs.

Some things never change, especially a Ferrari. The 1995 355 Berlinetta evidenced a few structural changes but was still low-slung, flat-nosed, bright red, and outrageously expensive.

## DOWN THE ROAD

More so perhaps than in any other industry, automakers are concerned with the future development of their product. Even as a new model leaves the assembly line, company engineers are refining and developing ideas which will ultimately take the form of a vehicle more advanced in design and capability.

The Acura CL-X coupe is a silvery bullet due for general sale in 1997. A projectile-like nose with slanted, inlaid headlights and a broad, wraparound windshield set at a rakish backward angle give it the look of something out of "Star Trek."

Still in experimental form, the Buick XP2000 sedan is intended to be a high-tech communications center on wheels. The hood section is flat and vented, with oblong headlights and a sloped profile implying power and drive.

But leave it to the Germans to do something totally innovative: Mercedes-Benz engineers are designing a modular vehicle composed of interchangeable parts. Depending upon their arrangement it is possible to have a coupe, convertible, station wagon, or pickup at one's disposal, as the occasion dictates.

The Mitsubishi 3000GT VR-4 is now available on the American market in a spyder version with the only existing retractable rigid roof. A collapsible top lifts up and back for deposit in a rear compartment.

Hyundai's new mini-4 x 4 is a canary-yellow confection with a lot of glass and a tailgate which opens from the middle of the roof down, giving the rear end a sharklike appearance.

*The trademark of the 1996 Dodge Viper is the guttural roar of its powerful V-10 engine. It has all the capabilities of a real dragster and no passenger amenities worth mentioning. Ear plugs are recommended.*

Mixing space and art-deco concepts, Ford engineers have come up with a GT 90 sports car which boasts a V-12 engine. Its nose—an expansive, curved fender housing retractable headlights—rises to a domed cockpit of glass. This is truly a car that Buck Rogers would be proud to own.

Also all fenders and curves is the 1997 Pontiac GPX Grand Prix. The hood has a sleek convex sweep to it, with a pair of "nostril" vents positioned near the nose. In the driving compartment is a dashboard resembling that of a jetliner.

The Chrysler Atlantic possesses the lines and appearance of the famous Bugatti models of bygone years. Some observers go so far as to say that it bears a striking resemblance to the 1958 Jaguar XK 150 roadster, only with a hardtop.

Once abandoned and now resurrected, the Lamborghini Cala lives on as a sleek, glassy prototype with great potential and a strong prospective market. Possessed of a low, sweeping shape and a jutting backside air foil, the experimental model displays a nose-to-the-ground stance reminiscent of a road racer. It's projected to have a 320-horsepower engine and a flexible suspension system to compensate for insufficient ground clearance.

Nothing is so constant as change, and the automotive industry is a classic case in point. Yet sports cars—and all cars—must maintain strong fantasy appeal in order to stimulate sales. As ego and image continue to influence human nature, dream car fever will persist as the happy malady of motorists everywhere.

*The 1994 Lamborghini Diablo VT assumed something of an aristocratic air with a midnight black exterior—but in the driving compartment the quarters were cramped, making it difficult to work the pedals properly.*

In 1994 the Ford Mustang
experienced a much publicized
redesign—the resulting changes
are readily evident in the MPM
P-51 convertible model of that year.

*The 1995 Ferrari 355 Spyder was classified as a street-legal racer. Engineers did everything to enhance its speed, including a flat Formula One undercarriage and a light steel-aluminum body.*

*A work of engineering art, the 1994 Porsche Speedster featured leather reclining bucket seats, dual air bags, a theft-deterrent system, locking pressure-cast light alloy wheels, and Tiptronic, a driver information center.*

*The 1994 Toyota Supra Twin Turbo came with dual air bags and four wheel anti-lock brakes. Its six-cylinder in-line engine and a six-speed manual transmission gave it strong acceleration. Bucket seats marked a nice interior design.*

*As were its predecessors, the 1994 Pontiac Firehawk was a street-legal racer. A specially constructed powertrain and suspension system enabled it to post very respectable quarter mile times under racing conditions.*

*The 1995 Chevrolet Corvette did nothing to diminish this model's reputation as the best sports car in the world. Its acceleration slip regulator system provided sensational traction control under adverse road conditions.*

*True to its genre, the 1995 Ferrari F355 Berlinetta was a powerful vehicle aimed at drivers who liked speeds in excess of 100 miles per hour. It had a healthy price tag and creature comforts were at a minimum.*

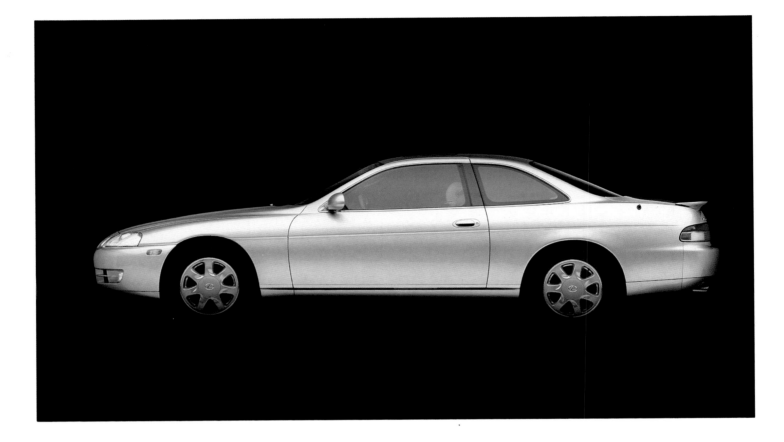

A luxury coupe, the 1995
Lexus SC 400 featured
dual air bags, automatic
transmission, and a big 4-
liter V-8 engine. It received
top marks for handling
and safety factors as
well as passenger comfort.

Still the car for those
who enjoy life in the fast
lane, the 1995 Chevrolet
Corvette appropriately
served as the official
pace car for the famous
Indianapolis 500-Mile
Memorial Day race.

*True to its illustrious Grand Prix heritage, the 1995 Lotus Esprit S4S displayed strong racing lines and a truncated backside complete with air foil. It continues to be one of the finest sporting cars on the market.*

*The 1995 Chevrolet Camero convertible was among the best handling and safest intermediate cars on the road that year. It came with dual air bags and a manual transmission as standard equipment.*

Management's continuing dedication to modern design and function were evident in the 1995 XJS Jaguar droptop. It was larger and heavier than the competition and sold more as a town car than a freeway cruiser.

The 1995 Trans Am continued to be Pontiac's most powerful sports car, with a variety of new options available ranging from traction control to fog lamps. Its design was strictly futuristic.

*FOLLOWING PAGE:*
*The 1995 Ford Saleen Mustang S351 kept abreast of the competition with improvements to steering and suspension systems that made for better handling, particularly at higher speeds.*

The 1995 Mercedes Benz 500SL provided the ultimate experience in convertible driving. Auto experts generally agree that nothing in the droptop line quite compared to the 500SL in stability, refinement, prestige, and price, calling the model a triumph of German engineering.

The 1996 Porsche 911 Twin Turbo holds forth as one of the fastest cars in the world. It can go from start to 60 miles per hour in an eye-popping 3.5 seconds. And its top speed is in the 177 mph range—definitely not for amateurs.

The 1996 Dethomaso Guara is a futuristic concept car utilizing the fiery red veneer and curved lines so reminiscent of a late model Ferrari. But its design most closely resembles that of the Lamborghini Cala.

*The 1990 Lamborghini Countach, the company's twenty-fifth anniversary model, was the last of this line to be produced. Due to its size the Countach was difficult to maneuver on Europe's narrow country roads and so gave way to a more modern design.*

*Sleek and sporty, the 1996 BMW Z3 Roadster is the smallest of the German manufacturer's line but certainly not the least in performance. It can reach 113 miles per hour and has a very respectable acceleration capability.*

*Despite a relatively narrow wheel base, the 1996 BMW Z3 Roadster corners well and holds the road acceptably under all but the most adverse conditions.*

*Like other members of its breed the 1994 Lamborghini Diablo VT was big, heavy, and extremely powerful. At top speeds the driver had to be strong of arm to steer properly and not be easily intimidated by the task.*

*The 1995 Porsche Carrera 993-C2 was specifically designed for experienced drivers. It grips the road less tenaciously than the other Porsche models and allows drivers the pleasure of using their skills to control the action.*

# INDEX

Page numbers in **bold-face** type indicate photo captions.